Con

CONTENTS ....

INTRODUCTION 3

WHY OXBRIDGE? 4

WHAT ARE OXBRIDGE INTERVIEWERS REALLY LOOKING FOR? 7

WRITING YOUR PERSONAL STATEMENT 12

WHAT IS BACKGROUND READING? 15

HOW DO I KNOW WHAT TO READ? 17

OTHER WAYS TO DEMONSTRATE YOUR INTEREST.............20

CURRENT AFFAIRS AND GENERAL KNOWLEDGE 22

ANALYSING YOUR PERSONAL STATEMENT 23

MOCK INTERVIEWS 29

MOCK INTERVIEW CRIB SHEET 32

HOW TO APPROACH AN INTERVIEW QUESTION 33

ATTENDING THE INTERVIEW 37

WHAT HAPPENS NEXT? 40

ACTION CHECKLIST...42

Introduction

I deliberately set out to write a short book. There's no point you spending more time reading about how to prepare for your Oxbridge interview than actually doing the preparation.

I also set out to write an encouraging book. Your interviewer is not coming down from on high to judge you and your entire life forever. They want to see if you are the sort of person they would enjoy having at their college for three years. That's all.

Finally, I set out to write a practical book with specific instructions. It's all very well telling you to do lots of background reading and giving example questions. But how do you know what to read? And what if they don't ask you those questions? Follow the advice contained herein and you will have done all you reasonably can to prepare yourself.

Good luck!

Why Oxbridge?

Although interviewers are no longer allowed to ask you why you applied to that college, it's good to know for yourself why you want to apply to Oxbridge at all – if indeed you actually do. Many people end up applying because they are told they ought to because they are predicted good A Level results, because that's what clever pupils do, because it will make the school (or their parents) look good.

The difference between Oxbridge and most other universities is principally the speed and intensity of learning. It is, of course, staffed by world-renowned experts in every department, but there are world-renowned experts at other universities too – and there's no guarantee you'll end up being taught by one! What all subjects and courses at Oxbridge have in common is that you will do an awful lot of work.

Terms are eight weeks long, and with few exceptions you will be doing a single-honours degree. That is, studying only one subject. You will have one or more supervisions/tutorials a week, for which you will be required to write an essay, solve problems, or do an equivalent amount of work. You will then be grilled (either alone or in a small group) about the work you have produced for an hour, with nowhere to hide the gaps in your thinking. At some universities, you might do this once a term. At Oxbridge, therefore, you might do more hands-on work in one term than some people do in their entire degree.

You are also assessed predominantly by exam. You will probably write a dissertation and may choose some paper which require 'long essays' (two or more essays which in total add up to roughly a dissertation in length, but you will also take a lot of exams. This is why A Level results are so important. If you can't score highly in a A Level exam, you will struggle to score highly in the exam-dominated Oxbridge system.

You will also be an environment where pretty much everyone was top of their class at school. You will, I'm afraid, be a very small fish in your new academic pond! This can come as quite a blow to one's self-esteem, and it is better to get over comparing yourself with your university peers as quickly as possible. It won't make your supervisions any less excruciating: only enough hours in the library will do that.

Contact time (both indirect in lectures and direct in supervisions/tutorials) will vary by course, but you will certainly spend a lot more time alone. This is what self-directed learning really means. Can you discipline yourself to spend the time actually studying, and do you have the ingenuity to work out what the question means and where you might find some help answering it?

But if you are interested in pushing yourself to the limit intellectually, and if you are yearning to be surrounded by people who are full of energy, ambition and enthusiasm for all areas of life (whether it be music, sport, theatre, or ultimate frisbee), then you can do nothing better upon leaving school than spending three years at one of the best universities in the whole world: Oxford or Cambridge.

What are Oxbridge interviewers really looking for?

In order to understand the Oxbridge interview process, you need to understand the criteria that interviewers use to select their future students – because that it what it's about, not a judgement on your worth as a human being. Your interviewer, or one of their close colleagues, will spend three years reading your drivel and trying to help you develop a rigorous and critical brain. Because no matter how well you did at school, you will start off writing repetitive, naïve drivel. Sorry. Oxbridge really is a different ball game.

What they are looking for is not just someone who can uphold the ancient academic traditions of Oxbridge but someone with whom they can bear to spend a lot of time over the next three years discussing half-formed adolescent ideas, and who might stand a chance at coming out the other end a decent thinker. There's no need for you to impress them at this stage. In fact, can you truly imagine impressing one of the foremost academics in your subject in the whole world with something you read while doing your A Levels?

All this is not to say for one moment that you shouldn't apply and give it your all. Actually, it is an encouragement to do so because you don't need to be unique or superlative to pass an Oxbridge interview. You just need three things. (And if you don't have them, seriously, you might actually be happier somewhere else.)

Passion

I'm sure you've heard this one. Sometimes it seems that unless you live and breathe your subject and forsake food and water in order to grasp a single tiny kernel of understanding. How many people do you think actually live like that? I'll give you a clue: far fewer than the total undergraduate population of Oxbridge.

Throughout your school career, you will have focused in on an increasingly narrow range of subjects. You'll have dropped some when you started your GCSEs, more when you started your A Levels, and now you're being asked to choose just one thing to spend 100% of your "working" week on for three years.

It is true that compared to other universities, Oxbridge is _hard_. Work hard, play hard. You'll be churning stuff out non-stop for eight weeks then try to collapse sufficiently during the vacation to haul yourself upright and do it all again the next term.

Do you have sufficient interest in your subject to work on it and nothing else for sixty hours a week? It doesn't have to be your whole life, but you have got to be able to put the hours in without getting bored. Your interviewer does not want someone who is going to change subjects five minutes in or drop out because they want to do other things.

If you're not actually interested in your chosen subject…don't apply for it! Do something else! A different subject, a gap year, an apprenticeship…anything! Don't sign yourself up for three years of trying to dredge up an interest in something you actually find boring or pretentious.

Intelligence
There's no two ways about it: you've got to be bright. But you don't have to be a genius. Virtually no one is a genius at your age – it takes a lot of practice - that's why child prodigies are a thing. To get into Oxbridge, you just need to be intelligent _enough_.

You have got to get top grades at A Level. Even if you succeed in the interview, if you don't get stellar grades then you won't make your offer. Ask your teachers whether they think you're working at the right level to get top grades. If not? Focus on the areas in which you seem weakest, and ask them what you can do to improve. You need to put the work in yourself, rather than being hauled along by tutors. If you can't manage A Levels, you'll sink rather than swim at Oxbridge.

But you also need to have a curious mind. Are you fundamentally interested in finding things out? About your chosen subject, of course, but also about the world generally. This cannot be taught per se, but it can be developed. Much like A Levels, it's a bit late to start from scratch now, but you can work on it.

The best possible thing you can do is to read. Read books (fiction and non-fiction), read the newspapers, read controversial blogs… Challenge yourself. Read something you know nothing about. Read the latest bestseller. Read the top three classic novels of all time. Read poetry. However, make an effort to read long-form things. Much of the world today is delivered in bite-sized pieces which are too small to get into any subject in adequate depth, and can only give a single perspective. Books and long articles are far better for practicing taking an idea and following it through.

Teachability

You are not expected to know everything as soon as you get to university. In fact, it would be ridiculous if you did! Why would you bother doing a degree? Interviewers want to see that you have both the intellectual agility and the humility to have new ideas thrown at you, to form well-justified opinions about those ideas, and to have your own opinions torn apart and thrown right back at you again. It can be very dispiriting to have laboured all week on an essay and to then have your supervisor/tutor immediately expose what a load of unfounded bluster it is. If you can get up from that with a smile and immediately start talking again, you'll do alright.

To become more teachable, you must first know your place. Your interviewer has spent years delving into their field. You haven't even left school. If they say something, pay attention. If they ask a question, there must be a reason. Find it. But don't just roll over like a doormat. If they don't want someone to talk back at them, they can write a book. It's a discussion, not an adversarial debate.

Second, books on critical thinking abound. They will explain to you how to argue logically and how to spot the flaws in someone else's argument. Emotive opinions count for nothing in the rationalist melee of a university.

Writing your personal statement

You will, no doubt have received plenty of advice on writing your personal statement. There are innumerable books and websites with guidelines and examples, and it seems everyone has a different opinion about how many books you should include, how much space to devote to extracurricular activities, and cunning ways to get the character count down.

I won't go into that here, but I will explain how the personal statement fits into the context of the Oxbridge interview. If you write yours for Oxbridge it will do for everywhere else you're applying, and if you write it and use it correctly then you won't accidentally shoot yourself in the foot.

As your interviewer sits in the room awaiting you, they will have your UCAS application to hand. They will know your GCSE results, which A Levels you are studying, your teacher's reference…and no doubt they will be re-reading your personal statement to prepare themselves to interview you. For Oxbridge, the rest of your application demonstrates that you meet the minimum requirements to be considered. It is the personal statement where they can begin to discern whether you as an individual would suit three years of rigorous study of a single subject at their college.

How will your personal statement help them do that?

First, your personal statement will simply be a conversation starter. Many interviewers may have lists of set questions, or short texts that they will ask you to read, but many more will prefer a freeform, conversational style. It means they can tailor the conversation to your interests and theirs, and needn't worry about unfairly asking about subjects which some interviewees have studied before and some haven't. But they have to break the silence somehow!

Asking initial questions based on your personal statement can make the first few minutes more comfortable for both of you. You won't be thrown in at the deep end just when you're at your most nervous, and they won't have to spend a lot of time wondering what to ask you. They can just look at your personal statement, pick something they're interested in, and see what you have to say about it.

Second, it does also give them a quick way to check out your credentials – to see that the claims you have made about yourself, your abilities and your interests are genuine. Anyone could write down an impressive list of books that they have read, but a few questions about anything mentioned on your personal statement will soon show whether you actually understood it. If you claim to have a huge passion for a particular area of your subject but cannot answer even the simplest question about it, that's a pretty obvious red flag that you're all talk and no walk.

Third, it will give them the chance to ask about something you know about already. Your first impressions of a new text or a new problem are interesting, but during your degree you will be pushed far beyond that. If they can pick a topic where they know you have a solid grounding already, they will be able to skip ahead quickly to the difficult questions and see how you fare at the advanced end (where they want you to spend your time) rather than needing to waste precious time getting there. This means, as we will discuss again later, that you need to know everything on your personal statement absolutely inside out and back to front. They will assume that the reason you've put it on there is that you are hoping they will ask you about it so you can discuss it in great detail. If you are truly shaky on the books and topics you've flagged up to them as your preferred conversation starters, they can't hold out much hope that you'll be able to cope with a large volume of difficult new material at a quick pace – which is what an undergraduate Oxbridge degree is.

Your personal statement, therefore, should contain the following things:

1. What you find most interesting about the subject for which you are applying
2. Specific references to extracurricular background reading and what you thought about it
3. Flagging up any areas of your A Levels which are particularly relevant
4. Anything particularly impressive you have done outside the classroom

The third section should be the biggest. Read on to find out how to gather material for it.

What is background reading?

As soon as you start thinking about applying to Oxbridge, you'll hear the phrase "background reading" everywhere. It is basically just anything academic you read outside your A Levels that is relevant to your subject. However, although we'll look at other ways to demonstrate your interest in your subject outside school, reading books is at the core of successful interview preparation. It is what you will spend most of your degree doing, and is therefore what the interviewer wants to check you are capable of and enjoy.

Passion

At school, you spread your time around a number of different subjects, and much of your learning time is highly controlled – either within a classroom or with set homework assignments. Background reading shows that you do actually have enough of an interest in your subject to spend your leisure time on it too. Spending three years on a single subject where most of your learning will be self-motivated is difficult! The interviewer wants to check that you'll be able to cope with it without getting bored – for your sake as much as for theirs! They don't enjoy teaching unmotivated students but they also don't want to inflict themselves on you if you're not excited to be there.

Intelligence

For someone applying to Oxbridge, A Levels should not be extremely difficult. Of course you will have to work hard, but you should be predicted excellent grades without flogging yourself to death. Reading outside your A Level course at a higher level demonstrates a higher level of intellectual ability. Your interviewer may well ask you to summarise a book you have read, as they won't have read everything there is on the subject, or might not have read it for a long time. Being able to give a concise and coherent explanation of the main arguments of an academic book goes a long way to showing that you will be able to digest the texts you will read as part of your degree.

Teachability

Whether your interviewer has read something or not, they will want you to give your considered, intellectual opinion on it. Then, they will try to rip it apart. They want to see that you can be challenged on something and come back with coherent responses and arguments. Or, if it becomes apparent that you have not considered something adequately, to rethink your position and engage in ongoing analysis. You will, of course, know all the background reading on your personal statement very well, so your response to your treasured opinions being torn to pieces will show your interviewer a great deal about how you would cope with a supervision/tutorial.

How do I know what to read?

When confronted with everything that's ever been written about your subject, it can be difficult to know where to start – and to know what will help you demonstrate passion, intelligence and teachability.

Ask a teacher
If you are doing an A Level in your proposed degree subject or a closely-related one, you can ask your subject teacher to recommend something to get you started. Choose the topic that you're most interested in and say you'd like to read more about it – what do they suggest? As they ought to know your capabilities reasonably well, hopefully they can point you to something (perhaps in the school library) that will be one level above where you are now.

Paper reading lists
Many faculties will have reading lists for their papers (like modules) online, and some will publish an introductory reading list for students to get stuck into the summer before they come up. Simply Google "Oxford/Cambridge [subject] reading list" and see if anything appears from the faculty website. If it has, you've struck a gold mine! Have a quick look a pick something that sounds interesting but not too specific. Anything with the word "Short", "Introduction" or "Concise" in the title will probably be a good place to start. However, a word of caution: you are almost guaranteeing that your interviewer knows that book like

the back of their hand and has discussed it a thousand times. If you're going to put it on your personal statement, you must feel like you have something to say about it.

Very Short Introductions
There is a lengthy series, published by Oxford University Press, of books called "A Very Short Introduction To…" They are, as you might guess, small books, but are written by the foremost academics in their field to be understood by the general public. You might even find one written by the person who is interviewing you! They will provide you with a overview of the topic but, crucially, will also have suggestions for further reading.

Faculty profiles
If you go to the website of the faculty to which you are applying, you will usually be able to find a list of academic or research staff. They will often have a little profile for each faculty member which includes books and journal articles which they have recently published. Many of these will be overly specialised for a pre-undergraduate, but you may well find something in the "Short", "Concise" or "Introduction" vein. You must, however, be extremely careful about reading anything by the person who is interviewing you. You will come across as extremely arrogant or ignorant if you try to tell them what their own work is really about!

Bibliographies

Once you've read your first book, however, the world is your oyster. Any academic book ought to have a bibliography and/or copious citations. You can be confident that almost any book in the bibliography will be equally academic and suitable, so just have a flick through and pick something else that sounds interesting.

<u>Other ways to demonstrate your interest</u>

None of the below is a substitute for background reading. Books are still the way in which you will do most of your learning at Oxbridge and in which you will demonstrate your intelligence and teachability. But they can be a useful addition if there are high-quality options available, and can go a long way towards demonstrating your passion and give your brain a workout in a different way.

Lectures
If there is a university near you, you may be able to attend public lectures. Some of these are free, others may have a small charge. You may also find lectures broadcast online or on the radio. TED talks, while useful for presenting challenging ideas and shaking you up a bit, should not be confused with an academic lecture.

Youtube
Depending on your subject, there may be some quality material on Youtube. Look for channels from venerable institutions such as the British Library or the Wellcome Trust. Be wary on mentioning this on your personal statement, but feel free to bring up an example in your interview – as long as you're clear that it was from a respected source, not a teenager in their bedroom.

Blogs

Blogs will be of more use to subjects which have obvious real-world application, such as medicine or economics. Don't cite them as serious sources, but they can be useful for exposing you to contrasting points of view or to currently contentious topics in your field.

Clubs

You can't really avoid the lure of the school club for your personal statement, but don't bother going into detail. Do it, especially if you can be club president, but know that every single other person being interviewed will also have run the French Film Club or the Debating Society.

MOOCs

Many universities now run Massive Open Online Courses. Most of them are beginner level, and make sure you don't compare them to a real degree course, but if you can find a free one that's good quality it may give you a good grounding in an area of your subject.

Current affairs and general knowledge

As part of your interview preparation, you should get into the habit of reading a newspaper every day. You don't have to read the whole thing cover to cover, but reading the major stories and a few opinion pieces in a good quality broadsheet will keep you abreast of what is going on in the world. Alternatively, pick a quality Sunday paper and read the whole thing.

As we have discussed, the Oxbridge interview is not a test of what you know, but being on top of current affairs can be invaluable in providing real-world examples for your answers, as well as helping you to give the impression of being generally curious and engaged in the world. Real-world examples are much more compelling than hypothetical ones, and choosing something from the current headlines means your interviewer will probably know it too and you can have an in-depth discussion about it.

Which newspaper to choose? I would suggest The Guardian/Observer, The Times, The Independent or The Telegraph. You could also consider a subscription to The Economist, The London Review of Books or The Spectator – but only if you're really going to get enough use out of them.

Analysing your personal statement

Once you've submitted your UCAS form, your work has only just begun. As you know by now, the personal statement essentially tells your interviewer what you would like to talk about in your interview. You mustn't allow yourself to be caught out by it!

Between submitting your form and your interview, try to avoid reading anything new. Your interviewer won't bring it up as they won't know you've read it, and the odds of working anything concrete like an actual book title or author into your interview answers in a genuinely relevant way are minimal. Focus now on depth, not breadth. Re-read anything you are unsure about. Far better to talk deeply about one book (i.e. at a level approaching degree level) than shallowly (as in A Levels) about many. You won't have time to cover everything you have read in your interview anyway, so better to know what you do know very thoroughly.

What you must do now is to take your personal statement and divide it into assertions (or claims, or ideas). By this I mean to separate out each individual thing that you say in your personal statement, so that you can look at them individually. You can either write them out in a document with each assertion as a section header, or format them into a table with the assertions in the first column and a second blank column.

For example:

With so many environmental tipping points approaching and many contentious issues surrounding the environment, there can seem to be little prospect of a fulfilling career in conservation. However, I strongly feel that science has the potential to produce a sustainable planet if people are educated to understand its value.

Would become:

With so many environmental tipping points approaching
and many contentious issues surrounding the environment,
there can seem to be little prospect of a fulfilling career in conservation.
However, I strongly feel that science has the potential to produce
a sustainable planet
if people are educated to understand its value.

Or:

I am captivated by the diversity and depth offered by a History degree; attracted by the way it encourages us to be analytical of the values and patterns of past societies.

Would become:
I am captivated by the diversity and depth offered by a History degree;
attracted by the way it encourages us to be analytical
of the values
and patterns of past societies.

Once you have done this, and have a rather long list of headings or first column of a table, you must go through each assertion and write down everything you can think of that you might talk about in relation to it. Try to challenge yourself to find evidence to back your statement up, and examples you might use.

For example:

With so many environmental tipping points approaching – name three. When are they expected? What is the evidence for them? Have any passed already?

and many contentious issues surrounding the environment, - name three. Why are they contentious? Which side do you fall on? What evidence do you have to support your assessment?

there can seem to be little prospect of a fulfilling career in conservation. – then why are you studying it? What made you change your mind?

However, I strongly feel that science has the potential to produce – why? What potential? Why hasn't it done it already?

a sustainable planet – define both sustainable and planet.

if people are educated to understand – how are people to be educated? Doesn't everyone know about climate change these days? Why aren't we doing more to tackle it?

its value. – what is its value? What evidence do you have for this?

Or:

I am captivated by the diversity and depth offered by a History degree; - surely all degrees are diverse and deep? What are you most looking forward to studying?

attracted by the way it encourages us to be analytical – how do we analyse history differently from other subjects? Can you give three examples of this?

of the values – name three. Name three things that are unique about each of them.

and patterns of past societies. – name three. Name three things that are unique about each of them.

Any sentence, clause or even sub-clause or perhaps even word in your personal statement might be used as the basis of a long, in-depth, high-level academic discussion. Are you ready for that? For *any* part of your personal statement to be the opening question?

To help you, here are some generic questions to ask yourself to get started:

1. For each significant noun, can I define it? If relevant, can I give three examples? Can I say why each of them is important?
2. If you have said that anything is 'interesting' (or 'fascinating' or 'captivating' or any other synonym), be very sure you can explain why.
3. If you mention a book, can you describe the book's contents in a few sentences? In more detail? The same for any other media.
4. If you mention a person, who are they? When did they live and work? What did they do?
5. If you mention part of your A Level syllabus, can you talk about it for five minutes straight? Is there any part of it which you don't fully grasp?
6. What did you learn from any of your extracurricular activities? What are your plans

for them next? Are they related to your subject? Why are you interested in them?

7. Is there anything you are hoping they will ask about? Why?
8. Is there anything you are hoping they won't ask about? Why not?

You will probably notice that there are some gaps – some of your statements have less supporting evidence than others. This is to be expected – fear not! However, you have now identified for yourself the areas where you need to do some more reading and thinking. You can make yourself a to-do list (e.g. re-read the book you realise you can't remember well, find some examples of cases where something is true and not true…) based on your personal statement analysis and spend the time between submitting your form and the date of your interview going through it.

It is worth prioritising this interview preparation over your A Level studies. I'll say it again: active, focused interview preparation is more important than doing your A Level homework. Your exams are some time away. You can always catch up. You're clever. Your interview is soon. You can't cram for it.

If necessary, it is worth saying to your A Level teachers that you would like to spend more time preparing for your Oxbridge interview, so please would they be understanding if your work isn't quite up to scratch until it's over. It's not an excuse to not turn up to classes or to not hand in homework at all, but you may need to spend less time on it in order to make time to read up for your interview.

How much time? Well, how long is a piece of string. However, half an hour every weekday would be a good starting point. Maybe you have an awkward single free period (sorry, 'study period') you could allocate to Oxbridge prep. Maybe you get up earlier and do it first thing in the morning, or do it immediately when you get home from school. If you can't do it on some days, try to catch up at the weekend, although it's better to pace yourself. Think of this as starting to learn self-discipline for the independent study you will be doing at university.

Your task is simply to flesh out your personal statement analysis. First, fill in the gaps. Then see if you can delve deeper. As you read more, add it to your document. Eventually it will be many pages long! Try to make your notes concise – they are aides memoire rather than an essay in and of themselves. After all, you won't be writing your interview – you'll be speaking it.

Mock interviews

You'll have spent a lot of time reading and writing about your A Level subjects by now, but probably very little time talking about them out loud. This is the place where most interviewees trip up. You don't just need to know your personal statement and everything on it inside out – you need to be able to talk intelligently and articulately about it. You need to be able to produce coherent sentences (verbal paragraphs, even) and speak them with a reasonable level of confidence (at least to the extent that your thoughts aren't smothered with "ums" and "ers" and they are actually audible) and explain each step of your thought process as you answer a question which will probably be quite challenging. Now is the time to stop studying and start talking.

Your school may be able to arrange a formal mock interview for you. If they don't offer, try asking your subject teacher (or one in a similar subject) if they would mind doing one for you one lunchtime or after school. You should give them a copy of your personal statement in advance and treat the whole process as if it were the real thing. Wear the clothes you are planning to wear if you can, shake their hand when you come into the room, and use appropriately academic language.

Even if you can have a formal mock interview, it will be helpful to have some additional informal practice. Thinking out loud and giving immediate answers to complex questions is quite different from writing things out in an exam hall, so the more time you can spend doing it the better. You don't need your "interviewer" to be an expert in your subject. In fact, they barely need to know anything about it at all. Recruit a friend or family member and give them your personal statement and the list of questions overleaf. If they don't understand anything you say, they should ask you to clarify. Clear speech reflects clear thought.

You can also practice alone. Set a timer for five minutes and pick one of the assertions from your personal statement analysis. Sit in a chair, as you will be in your interview, and talk about it at a normal conversational volume without notes for five minutes. Your interview answers certainly won't be five minutes long, but you will practice speaking your thoughts out loud and forming sentences correctly as you go.

The point at which you feel like you have run out of things to say is often the most valuable, as it is to that boundary of your current knowledge that your interviewer will try to push you. You must keep speaking until the timer goes off, so you must find something else to say that is reasonably connected to the topic at hand without dissolving into bluster. Argue against yourself. Find other examples. Conjecture about how it might have been different, or whether it could be in the future. Discuss the ways in which it is similar to and different from something else. You will feel like an idiot, although the odds are that you'll actually be saying something much more interesting than whatever you started off with. This is excellent practice for your entire academic career.

Mock interview crib sheet

Give this page and your personal statement to a parent or friend so they can do a mock interview. They can just fill in the blanks with things mentioned in your personal statement.

Can you summarise the main argument of [book]?
What do you think [person]'s most important contribution to [subject] is?
Tell me why you want to study [subject].
What has been your favourite part of your A Levels?
What are the major differences between [book] and [book]?
How are [person] and [person]'s work similar?
Why is [topic] interesting to students of [subject]?
Can you define [technical word]?
What bearing does [subject] have on [recent news item]?
Can you give me an example of [technical word] in something you have read?
How has [extra-curricular activity] made you think about [subject] differently?
What do you find most difficult to understand in [book]?
Is [anything!] relevant to [topic/subject]?
Did [book/topic/person] remind you of anything from your A Level studies?
Tell me more about [whatever you just said].

How to approach an interview question

Teachers often say there are no stupid questions so you can ask them anything. They are often lying, but it is true of interviewers. If they ask you a question, there must be something interesting to talk about – even if it seems banal or random.

You'll have heard horror stories about 'trick' questions in Oxbridge interviews. You can find dozens of examples on the internet. I'm sorry to say that there's nothing 'trick' about them. Usually you will find that they are taken out of context and came in the course of a quite normal discussion. Alternatively, they may have been deliberately chosen to be open-ended and allow you to interpret the question however you like. There is no magical answer that if you get it right will immediately mean you have passed with flying colours. They just want to see if you're able to say anything remotely relevant, interesting and coherent and then they'll go on from there.

For absolutely any question, you must say *something*. This might seem obvious now, but it's very easy to feel like a rabbit in the headlights and just mumble a few words. Or if they ask a question like "Is the moon made of green cheese?" to just say "No". It technically answers the question but isn't really an *answer*.

Most Oxbridge interview questions have an implied 'why?' or an implied 'can you give me an example?' The facts aren't the important things here because not everyone does the same curriculum. It's not a knowledge test – it's an intelligence and teachability test. Whatever you say, they're likely to either present a counter-argument/counter-example or to ask you to explain more about it. If you give the best, most perfect, most complete answer imaginable, they will still ask you more about it! They want to find the limit of your current knowledge and take you into new and uncharted territory to see how you cope with it. Wherever the boundary is, they'll take you a step further.

If you are totally thrown by a question which either seems completely random or that you know absolutely nothing about (e.g. What do you think [person you have never heard of] would say to that?), ask yourself three things:

1. Is this like something I have read or know?
2. Can I answer any part of the question?
3. Can I ask them a simple question to get some missing information?

For example…

"How could the Mars Rover test the surface of the moon to see if it was made of green cheese?"
You might know what the Mars Rover did on Mars (in terms of on-site testing, photography, sample-taking…) and talk about how that would be similar on the moon and how it would be different. Or you might know a test for cheese or a component of cheese (such as milk!)

and discuss whether it would be possible in a lunar atmosphere.

"What cultural and scientific implications would there be if the moon were made of green cheese?"
You might not have the slightest idea about culture, but perhaps you could think of some scientific implications. Landing the Mars Rover might be a bit stickier, for a start! You can always come back round to culture later.

"What do you think of Crispin-Buxley's theory that the moon is made of green cheese?"
You simply say that you haven't heard of that particular theory, but please could they explain it. They won't mind. There's no particular reason you should have done, unless you claim it in your personal statement. They will tell you what it is, briefly, and then you can start discussing what you do think.

As long as you're in an academic frame of mind, you shouldn't worry about saying what you really think, even if it's a bit left-field. You simply need to ensure the conversation keeps moving on and that you are in some way addressing the subject at hand.

For example, "Instead of politicians, why don't we let the managers of Ikea run the country? - my first thought is that they probably wouldn't want to! But as well as being a little joke, it does have serious bearing on the question. If Ikea managers wanted to be politicians they probably would be already, so you might assume that they are more interested in retail than in national issues – and isn't it important that we have people who are passionate about national issues trying to deal with them? If they are interested and invested they are likely to do a better job, and more likely to persevere and not leave for other jobs. (This might lead to a discussion on whether the amount someone is personally affected by an issue affects how well they can will legislate about it. Or about why politicians chose that career path. Or about whether lifetime career politicians are better or worse than someone with experience elsewhere.)

Remember, there is no right answer. The only wrong answer is no answer. Aim for roughly a 'paragraph' length for each answer – neither a single word or sentence, nor an essay that leaves them with no breathing room to ask questions.

Attending the interview

Be early
Plan to arrive half an hour before your interview. If travel times mean it's more convenient to arrive earlier, do it. There will be somewhere in the college you can wait, and you absolutely do not want to be rushing in at the last minute. It may be difficult to find your interview room – make sure you have enough time.

Wear something that you feel comfortable in that isn't distracting
You can wear anything you want to your interview, but do make sure it's something that will keep the interviewer focused on the conversation and not your clothes. You'd do better to avoid loud slogans and anything too outrageous. Jeans and a T-shirt is fine, a suit is fine, a dress is fine… whatever you like. The important thing is that you are physically comfortable (not constantly adjusting your collar or pulling down your skirt) and in the right frame of mind for an academic discussion. If you'll be at your sharpest in a tracksuit, that's no problem, but you might want to consider wearing something like a formal interview outfit or even your school uniform to help set the tone for yourself. A good mid-range combo for either sex is a shirt/blouse, trousers/a knee-length skirt, and a V-neck jumper.

Bring your personal statement analysis
Give it a read-through the night before and the
morning of, just so everything is fresh in your mind,
and you could also use it to while away the time before
your interview if you're nervous. But do put it away
before you go in!

**Shake your interviewer's hand and wait to be told
where to sit**
When you walk in, you might be confronted with more
than one interviewer and more than one chair. Shake
each interviewer's hand individually, looking them in
the eye and trying to smile, and then wait for the head
interviewer to indicate a chair to you. If they don't, just
point at one and say "Here?" It's not a test, you just
don't want to end up sitting weirdly close or far away,
or on a chair that they're expecting to use. Try to pick
one that's firmer and more upright if you do end up
having a choice – you're likely to feel a bit more poised
than on a big squashy sofa.

Take a breath and speak clearly
No matter how thrilling your thoughts, your interviewer
is going to have a hard time if they struggle to hear
them. Before you speak, take a proper breath in and
out. It'll give you a moment to collect yourself and also
make sure you've got enough air in your lungs to speak.
As part of your interview practice, you should make
sure you speak loudly and clearly. Look them in the eye

and don't mumble. There is absolutely no problem at all in having an accent – the point is simply to enunciate.

Try to seem enthusiastic!
Remember that you want to come across as passionate and teachable. The best interview will be one in which you do actually have fun. You're supposed to enjoy discussing your subject at a higher level, even though you might be quaking with nerves. You can practice your tone of voice and your expressions in mock interviews – either with someone else, in front of a mirror, or even in front of a video camera. Try to have a bit of energy rather than sitting there like a lump.

Make the most of your visit
You'll either have gaps between interviews or some time at the beginning and/or end of the day. Use it to wander around your college or faculty building, around the town more generally, and to speak to other people who are there for interviews or to current students. If you get in, you'll spend three years of your life here. Are you going to enjoy it?

<u>What happens next?</u>

You got in!

Congratulations! You'll probably get a letter before UCAS is updated. Now you just need to work hard to ensure you get your A Level grades.

You didn't get in.

Sorry. Bad luck. I have to reassure you, though, that this isn't personal and it isn't the end of the world. There are many other truly excellent universities in the country, and it is just the case that both Oxford and Cambridge have too many brilliant applicants to give them all places. Wallow in your sorrows briefly, by all means, but do pick yourself up and dust yourself off and keep going. You can have a great time and an excellent education anywhere.

You've been pooled.

This means that your first choice college did not have space for you but they believe you are good enough to be admitted to the university so they have put your application in a pool so that other colleges (who didn't get enough good applications) can look at it and perhaps offer you a place. This is great news! If you had a second interview at the same time as your first, that college will have first dibs on you if they have places available. If not, a college may take you on the strength of your UCAS application and interview notes alone, or they may call you back for an interview with them. It doesn't mean anything particular either way – it's just the way that college likes to work.

Action Checklist

- ☐ Read between three and five books of an appropriate level
- ☐ Start reading the news for fifteen minutes to half an hour a day
- ☐ If applicable, subscribe to a decent general publication (e.g. The Economist, the London Review of Books) or academic journal (if you're feeling brave)
- ☐ Write your personal statement. Include:
  - ○ What you find most interesting about the subject for which you are applying
  - ○ Specific references to extracurricular background reading and what you thought about it
  - ○ Flag up any areas of your A Levels which are particularly relevant
  - ○ Anything particularly impressive you have done outside the classroom
- ☐ Break down your personal statement into its component parts
- ☐ Write in bullet points anything that is relevant to each part
- ☐ Go back to your background reading or do more to fill in any bits that look thin
- ☐ Do at least two full half-hour mock interviews, either with a teacher, relative or friend
- ☐ Sit down and talk about a section of your personal statement for five whole minutes at least three times
- ☐ Pick your outfit (consider bringing a spare)

- [ ] Work out your travel times
- [ ] Attend interview
- [ ] Go nuts! Do something totally silly and non-academic to blow off steam.
- [ ] Wait.
- [ ] Wait some more.
- [ ] Nearly die of waiting.
- [ ] Receive letter… good luck!

Has this book been helpful?

Do me a favour – help me to help more people (and, obviously, sell more books.)

1. Leave a review on Amazon. Longer, balanced reviews are more helpful to other customers.
2. Buy a copy for a friend.
3. Mention it to your Head of Sixth Form, careers advisor or school librarian.

Printed in Great Britain
by Amazon